COSY

COMFORT

HAPPINESS

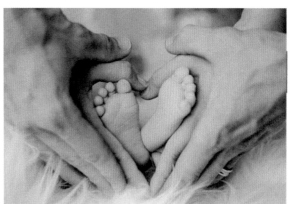

FIXED-RATE MORTGAGE

FAMILY

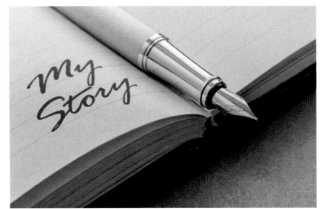

CALM
SPACE

MY

STYLE
Minimalist
DESIGN

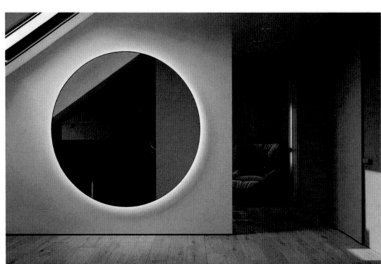

SIDE
VIEW

LAKE

FOREST
green area

BIG *City*

love **LIFE**

MODERN
interior

JUST
perfect
NOW

DREAM
BIG

FOCUS
ON
YOUR
GOALS

SEA
view

GOALS

1.

2.

3.

relation
point of view.
Confidence
trusting rela
stability, or

A goal
without
a plan is
just
a wish.

FRESH
START

perfect
HOUSE

SUCCESS

best
DEAL

NEGOTIATION

live
your
dream.

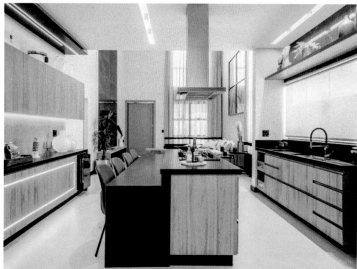

Thank you

for choosing our
DREAM HOME
Vision Board
Clip Art Book

Your feedback is essential to us
Please,
Let us know your opinion at

yonascopress@gmail.com

Much Love
Leen

Made in the USA
Las Vegas, NV
24 November 2024

12522699R00031